TAMAR

Also by Olajumoke Adenowo

Non-Fiction

Child of Destiny

Covenant Forces

Life Spring (The Mother's Prayer Manual)

Designed for Marriage

Mysterious Seed

Appointment with Destiny

Fiction

Beyond My Dreams

TAMAR

DESTINY ATTAINED AGAINST ALL ODDS
(BOOK THREE)

KINGDOM DYNAMICS FOR THE MARKETPLACE

OLAJUMOKE ADENOWO

Kingdom Dynamics for the Marketplace (Book Three)

TAMAR: Destiny Attained Against All Odds

ISBN 978-978-57390-1-5

Book Production, Design, & Printing:
Infospektra Publishing

Unless otherwise indicated, all scriptures are taken from the King James Version (KJV).

Contents

INTRODUCTION

Abraham begat Isaac; and Isaac begat Jacob; and Jacob begat Judas and his brethren; And Judas begat Phares and Zara of Tamar…
Mat. 1:2-3

I chose to make Tamar's story the last in this series even though she is the first woman mentioned in Matthew's account of the genealogy of Jesus. She is of tremendous encouragement to me because of her indefatigable pursuit of what she desired, ultimately her destiny.

There are two well-known Tamars in the Bible. Besides our protagonist, there was also the daughter of David, sister of Absalom, who was a victim of her half-brother's lust.

And it came to pass after this, that Absalom the son of David had a fair sister, whose name was Tamar; and Amnon the son of David loved her. And Amnon was so vexed, that he fell sick for his sister Tamar; for she was a virgin; and Amnon thought it hard for him to do anything to her.

But Amnon had a friend, whose name was Jonadab, the son of Shimeah David's brother: and Jonadab was a very subtil man. And he said unto him, Why art thou, being the king's son, lean from day to day? wilt thou not tell me? And Amnon said unto him, I love Tamar, my brother Absalom's sister. And Jonadab said unto him, Lay thee down on thy bed, and make thyself sick: and when thy father cometh to see thee, say unto him, I pray thee, let my sister Tamar come, and give me meat, and dress the meat in my sight, that I may see it, and eat it at her hand.

So Amnon lay down, and made himself sick: and when the king was come to see him, Amnon said unto the king, I pray thee, let Tamar my sister come, and make me a couple of cakes in my sight, that I may eat at her hand. Then David sent home to Tamar, saying, Go now to thy brother Amnon's house, and dress him meat. So Tamar went to her brother Amnon's house; and he was laid down. And she took flour, and kneaded it, and made cakes in his sight, and did bake the cakes. And she took a pan, and poured them out before him; but he refused to eat.

And Amnon said, Have out all men from me. And they went out every man from him. And Amnon said unto Tamar, Bring the meat into the chamber, that I may eat of thine hand. And Tamar took the cakes which she had made, and brought them into the chamber to Amnon her brother. And when she had brought them unto him to eat, he took hold of her, and said unto her, Come lie with me, my sister.

And she answered him, Nay, my brother, do not force me; for no such thing ought to be done in Israel: do not thou this folly. And I, whither shall I cause my shame to go? and as for thee, thou shalt be as one of the fools in Israel. Now therefore, I pray thee, speak unto the king; for he will not withhold me from thee. Howbeit he would not hearken unto her voice: but, being stronger than she, forced her, and lay with her.

Then Amnon hated her exceedingly; so that the hatred wherewith he hated her was greater than the love wherewith he had loved her. And Amnon said unto her, Arise, be gone. And she said unto him, There is no cause: this evil in sending me away is greater than the other that thou didst unto me. But he would not hearken unto her. Then he called his servant that ministered unto him, and said, Put now this woman out from me, and bolt the door after her. And she had a garment of divers colours upon her: for with such robes were the king's daughters that were virgins apparelled.

Then his servant brought her out, and bolted the door after her. And Tamar put ashes on her head, and rent her garment of divers colours that was on her, and laid her hand on her head, and went on crying. And Absalom her brother said unto her, Hath Amnon thy brother been with thee? but hold now thy peace, my sister: he is thy brother; regard not this thing. So Tamar remained desolate in her brother Absalom's house.

2 Sam. 13:1–19

From the story above, Tamar, David's daughter, was defeated by odds that seemed overwhelming. But our Tamar prevailed despite the travails she suffered. What could have been the secret to their differing outcomes? Both were exploited sexually by the existing male patriarchy, both were emotionally traumatised by male relatives. One ended up desolate in her brother's house, while the other, despite being conscripted to desolation in her father's house refused to give in to despair in spite of what she was subjected to. One ended up triumphant but the other did not.

We sometimes forget how young women like Ruth and Tamar would have been at the point we read of them in these stories. Their depths of wisdom and fortitude of character could have been nothing less than the invisible finger of God producing visible and eternal results in their lives.

The Bible refers to the promised land as the land of milk and honey. It is believed the honey referred to is the date syrup. Archaeologists and historians believe there was no honey in ancient Canaan. They were both called Tamar, 'date palm or palm tree'. Expectedly, they were created to be fruitful, produce sweetness, be extremely productive, and remarkably beneficial to mankind. This key component of the land of promise was a symbol of the promise of God. Yet the king's daughter's promised destiny was cut off when adversity struck while the maiden in our story prevailed.

We sometimes forget how young women like Ruth and Tamar would have been at the point we read of them in these stories. Their depths of wisdom and fortitude of character could have been nothing less than the invisible finger of God producing visible and eternal results in their lives. If under the old covenant they experienced such divine intervention, how much more would we who are under a better covenant based upon better promises?

But now hath he obtained a more excellent ministry, by how much also he is the mediator of a better covenant, which was established upon better promises.
Heb. 8:6

Are there principles the victorious Tamar put to work in her life which could have caused her to defy the odds? Can we put these same principles to work? As you keep your heart open while exploring her life, may her story be the catalyst needed to move you from where you are to where God has designed for you!

And Judah acknowledged them, and said, She hath been more righteous than I; because that I gave her not to Shelah my son. And he knew her again no more.

Genesis 38:26

Chapter 1

BAD THINGS HAPPEN TO GOOD PEOPLE

And Judah took a wife for Er his firstborn, whose name was Tamar.
Gen 38:6

Tamar's first wedding would no doubt have been an event filled with rejoicing, the starry-eyed bride naturally having great expectations and dreams. This day (as it is in many societies) was a dream come true of her parents and hers at once. What joy! Like at the cusp of every new venture, while she may have been anxious, faith triumphed over anxiety and she took a step into her future.

The family was being joined to that of the Hebrew patriarch, Isaac, who had settled in Canaan. His family was revered, had great wealth, and was feared. One of Isaac's sons,

Judah, had come to ask her father for her to be joined to his first son, Er. He had come with wonderful and breath-taking gifts which had awed the family and which they didn't refuse. It would be a great honour. As she prepared to leave, prayers were made for her that she would find joy in her new home and be fruitful. She was then taken to meet Er, and life with him began.

If you are suffering silently as the wife of a 'pleasant sadist', speak to someone trustworthy.

Judah's family was not what she expected it to be sadly. While Tamar had understood there would be adjustments she would have to make as a result of coming into a new family, new lifestyles and disciplines she would learn, what she had not expected was that her new family would seem very dysfunctional and her husband strange. The two sons of Judah were men who seemed devious and evil.

The first son, Er, was a wicked man as recorded in the Bible. His wickedness was such that God attested to it and had to snuff out his life.

And Er, Judah's firstborn, was wicked in the sight of the LORD; and the LORD slew him.

Gen. 38:7

Wickedness is a term used to describe certain individuals based on their actions. Whether or not they are deserving of the term is usually another matter.

There would be times where we would judge another's actions positively and call them terrific, or conversely feel they deserve to be punished, deserve death, or deserve to be treated a certain way. But unless you see from God's perspective and are privy to His thoughts, we may be walking in error in our judgment of another.

As the Bible says,

> *For my thoughts are not your thoughts, neither are your ways my ways, saith the LORD. For as the heavens are higher than the earth, so are my ways higher than your ways, and my thoughts than your thoughts.*
>
> **Isa. 55:8-9**

But unless you see from God's perspective and are privy to His thoughts, we may be walking in error in our judgment of another.

Calling an individual wicked is a term that is not meant to be used lightly. Is your husband as evil before God as you portray him to be? The boss you pray should die, are you sure you are praying God's heart? This may be why the judgment you expect or pray for hasn't come.

It is one thing for a man to call another evil. But when a God of overflowing mercy calls a man wicked, the man is who God says He is. God called Er wicked. This wasn't a sentimental woman's opinion, the envious prejudicial opinion of a competitor, the opinion of a troll in the media, or the decision of a jury. This was the verdict of the Judge of the whole earth!

This young woman must have experienced hell on earth. While Tamar must have experienced Er's evil firsthand, his death would still come as a shock. Being widowed at a young age was not what she had imagined. This had not been the plan. If her case was bad when he was alive, her case became terrible as a destitute widow in a patriarchal society.

I am so tired of hearing onlookers trying to adduce a reason to the sufferings of others.

Ancient society had its own safety net for such eventualities. Because Tamar had no children with Er, after his death she was given to his younger brother, Onan. This was the custom of many surrounding middle-eastern societies at the time, a custom later adopted and codified in the levirate mosaic law of marriage.

If brethren dwell together, and one of them die, and have no child, the wife of the dead shall not marry without unto a stranger: her husband's brother shall go in unto her, and take her to him to wife, and perform the duty of an husband's brother unto her.

Deut. 25:5

A male relative, usually a brother, was required to marry the widow of his relative. He would, with her, have seed who would be raised bearing the name of the departed. After the death of Er, Tamar was given to Onan. The children born would bear the name of the dead brother, Er, so he would not be forgotten.

And Judah said unto Onan, Go in unto thy brother's wife, and marry her, and raise up seed to thy brother.

Gen. 38:9

'And Judah said unto Onan…' This phrase in the verse above is very important. Some sources state that in pre-mosaic times, the responsibility for raising seed to his dead son was the father-in-law's. This Judah tried to do by sending Tamar to Onan. Bear this in mind as it would help to understand Tamar's actions later on.

When she realized she was going to have a second marriage,

I can imagine she hoped and prayed that life would be better with husband number two. Hopefully, this would be like the prayer we quote from Nahum 1:9 -

What do ye imagine against the Lord?
he will make an utter end: affliction shall
not rise up the second time.

The Bible and even history make it clear that bad things can happen to good people, to very good people. Even righteous and holy people approved of and loved deeply by God.

Now she would have a man who would care for her. Her days of mourning were over. Also, besides a decent husband, her seed would be birthed. The reproach of the scorners would finally cease.

After an official makes your life hell and he is moved from his role, it is logical to believe God has a better candidate in mind. Hope rises! Salvation has come finally. We begin to rejoice. Just like we would trust that God has changed our season for good if hope is birthed through any change at all after an extended period of suffering, Tamar too no doubt believed her lifting had come.

Her second wedding was a mere formality with no one invited. This was not the kind of news you announced from the rooftop or were proud to talk about. It wouldn't be a celebration of new beginnings or joy; it would be one of convenience, practicality, and expediency.

Onan didn't want to raise seed in his brother, Er's, name. This actually reveals a lot about their sibling relationships. The fact that he went along with the decision on the face of it but flouted the spirit and purpose of the act speaks to a twisted mind, one that was more concerned with hypocrisy and how he was perceived than true obedience. His actions could only have stemmed from a bitter and shrewd mind.

While he went about his duties on the surface as a husband before the world, marrying Tamar and regularly going in to sleep with her as agreed, he was merely exploiting her. He used her as a tool to satisfy his lust and assuage his appetite while depriving her of conception by spilling his seed on the floor. These encounters would have ended as soon as she got pregnant, but he prevented that from happening.

Tamar was frustrated. While she needed a child, Onan took his pleasure at her expense depriving her of the fruit of her endurance. I imagine she had to endure his touch simply because she was obeying the law and knew the purpose was to raise seed to Er's name. This was not what she expected, desired, and wanted for herself. We forget that in those times, women often had no say in these arrangements.

Onan knew he was not fulfilling the law, yet he was willing

to disobey God and frustrate the young widow than give his late older brother an offspring to bear his name. He was wicked indeed.

And Onan knew that the seed should not be his; and it came to pass, when he went in unto his brother's wife, that he spilled it on the ground, lest that he should give seed to his brother.

Gen. 38:9-10

Perhaps Onan was strategic and had a reason for what he did. The first child born to Er's widow would be deemed the heir of the deceased brother and entitled to claim the deceased brother's inheritance. The levirate child's inheritance, a double share to which the firstborn son is entitled, would go to Er. However, since he had died childless, his living brother Onan would be entitled to it along with what was already allotted to him. He would inherit Er's share and his if no child was birthed.

Onan was greedy and didn't want Tamar to conceive a son, a competitor who would take away the double portion from him. He wanted Er's double-portion along with his – a triple inheritance! He had probably rejoiced when Er died because he was now the oldest surviving son and next in line for all these inheritances.

Onan coveted and wanted to defraud the inheritance of the dead. This, I believe, was the real reason for his actions and why God slew him. How many people could Tamar tell what was going on in her inner sanctum? All people would see was that Onan was fulfilling the requirements while Tamar 'the barren' was yet again unfruitful in this second marriage too. Like in many societies, Tamar would be blamed for the failure of her husband.

Recently I have had to look at such issues through the lens of my work of fiction, **Beyond My Dreams**. The desolation and isolation suffered by wives of some men with good reputations, who are so pleasant in the eyes of society but mean and sadistic to their own spouses are devastating. Some of such men are leaders, and the women dare not speak to anyone of their husbands' behaviour as everyone views them as women to be envied. To whom would they complain? Yet true love and joy, the support and empathy which is the real fruit of their union with their husband, is non-existent.

I am not endorsing violence, but once in a while these women snap and commit acts of gross violence with fatal consequences and everyone gasps. Too many women have ended up in prison for acts committed while defending themselves. When these unfortunate incidences occur, there's an outcry! "Her husband is such a kind man! What else does she want?"

Let's not be so quick to judge others! No one knows what is going on in the secret lives of a married couple! If you are suffering silently as the wife of a 'pleasant sadist', speak to someone trustworthy. Don't die in pain, and Do Not commit a heinous act in response. Get help!

Tamar's dreams were broken. She wondered what kind of family she had been unfortunate to find herself in. Was Onan going to be this way all through the time she was his wife? Was she doing something wrong? Was something wrong with her? Maybe she needed to strive to do and be more so he could let her have the children she desperately desired. While she prayed and hoped for things to get better, suddenly he too was dead.

And the thing which he did displeased the LORD:
wherefore he slew him also.
Gen. 38:10

For Tamar, this was now husband number two dead. Note, God slew this husband also. You can be sure, although Onan was wicked, Tamar didn't immediately thank God for this judgment. In some societies, Tamar would have been viewed as a witch. What were the odds? The statistics looked really bad.

I am so tired of hearing onlookers trying to adduce a reason to the sufferings of others. They say for this calamity to occur, "She must have sinned" or at the very least "Maybe she didn't pray". Like the friends of Job, they engage mysteries they are not qualified to speak of. In the first place, it's not your business, and secondly, you don't have the entire picture. Thirdly, the Bible and even history make it clear that bad things can happen to good people, to very good people. Even righteous and holy people approved of and loved deeply by God.

Many are the afflictions of the righteous: but the
LORD delivereth him out of them all.
Psa. 34:19

Tamar's case was uncommon, and at this point Judah began to look at her strangely. The next line of action would have been for a third brother to marry her but this would have been no doubt a rare occurrence, and perhaps even unprecedented because by the second marriage, the widow should have been settled.

TAMAR
Destiny Attained Against All Odds

Then said Judah to Tamar his daughter in law, Remain a widow at thy father's house, till Shelah my son be grown: for he said, Lest peradventure he die also, as his brethren did. And Tamar went and dwelt in her father's house.

Gen. 38:11

Judah decided he would prefer to preserve his living son than raise a son in the name of the dead. He sent for Tamar and told her to return to her father's house. In other words, "Can you just return to your parents for a while? No, I don't think you have a problem. No, I don't think you are a witch. Just stay there until my third son is grown and then I will give you to him." He had no intention of ever giving her to Shelah. He thought she was what was known as a 'lethal woman', one whose partners died. However he said it, what he was now proposing to her was extremely shameful and dishonourable.

According to near-eastern customs from Middle Assyrian laws, if a man had no son over ten years old, he could perform the levirate obligation himself. We may not be able to grasp this through contemporary lenses considering this was before medical breakthroughs like artificial insemination. However, if the father-in-law chose not to, the woman is declared a widow, free to marry again.

Judah could have taken Shelah's place if Shelah was not old enough. He could also have set her free. But he does not. He sends her to live as a 'widow' in her father's house. He probably thought it was his way of punishing her for the deaths of his sons. It was deliberate and it was vindictive. She was to remain in limbo. Unlike other widows, she would not remarry and must stay chaste on pain of death. Judah seriously wrongs Tamar by this decision.

Naturally, it would become the talk of the town. She was the one who had no children, even though she had been married to two different men. She was also the one whose husbands had suddenly died mysteriously. If this was not news enough, everyone heard about how the family who came to ask for her hand in marriage and had happily welcomed her in a great celebration was now asking her to return to her father.

This was not the norm. Now she was a part of the family, her place - irrespective of her circumstances - was supposed to be retained and secure. It was one thing to be ashamed, embarrassed, and by herself while in her new family. But to be told to pack her things and leave was unexpected. Where would she return to? There was a likelihood there was no room anymore for her in her parents' home. But since Judah, her father-in-law, had given the command, she had no choice.

Tamar obeyed, took her things, and returned to her father.

... testings and trials needed for our shapings would come most times through human vessels.

The resilience, wisdom, and will needed to be all God intends would only come through many trials, just as gold can only be revealed through great fire. As with every one of us whom the Lord has called, the testings and trials needed for our shapings would come most times through human vessels. This was Tamar's experience.

Perhaps your journey into entrepreneurship, a career or new job started with great expectations and faith. This is right, this is needed. For without faith we can't take risks. In the words of Alexander the Great, "Fortune favours the bold". We do not wait until all the lights are green before setting out on a journey. After all the analysis, business plans, and feasibility studies, after finding out all we can about that new organization, at some point we must take a step of faith and start the business, or new job.

But like Tamar, have you ever found yourself taking a leap of faith into what you thought would be a rewarding experience only to find yourself in a regrettable position? How do you retain your sanity in the midst of constant evil and pain like Tamar had? She could have chosen to give it all up and return to her family at any point when she saw the kind of home she had been brought into. Yet she stayed. She could have also given in to despair and become broken in the process. But she retained her hope.

Also, as is usually the case, she could have chosen to become like them, also learning wickedness in a bid to outwit them or survive. Isn't that usually the quickest and easiest way we try to deal with the evil around us? Sometimes you are in a relationship where the other party is constantly unkind to you. Other times in business, you are faced with people who dream up one form of mischief or the other to make you sin or bring your business down. Do not give anyone permission to make you into who you are not. Keep your eyes and heart fixed on God and determine to retain your own righteousness.

There's a mystery about God's people of covenant. Though they may retreat, they do not reverse.

Have you ever experienced a reversal? It's tough. It's rough. It's the stuff of ridicule and scorn. There are some who take their own lives when they encounter setbacks. How those Tamar left behind on the day of her nuptials must have laughed! It appeared that she had suffered a terminal reversal.

But the path of the just is as the shining light, that shineth more and more unto the perfect day.
Pro. 4:18

There's a mystery about God's people of covenant. Though they may retreat, they do not reverse. They have been set fixedly on a path and plan already predestined by God. When you keep your eyes and heart on God, He promises your path will begin to shine brighter and brighter. That seeming siege, that seeming reversal is a smokescreen. You are about to fly farther and faster than ever before.

Even though His mercy is longsuffering and infinite, having the ability to preserve and keep alive, it can also slay and send destruction. God was so displeased with Onan and Er that, in mercy for humanity, He slew them. Every Pharaonic conspiracy desiring to stop you from birthing God's vision for your life will be destroyed in this season.

To him which smote great kings: for his mercy endureth for ever: And slew famous kings: for his mercy endureth for ever.
Psa. 136:17–18

And of thy mercy cut off mine enemies, and destroy all

them that afflict my soul: for I am thy servant.
Psa. 143:12

It is impossible for anyone to reverse the destiny of a child of God. Impossible. No situation has the capacity to bring you to a reversal. When the string of a bow is drawn by an expert archer, the farther he seems to draw that string backwards, the faster and farther the arrow would fly. Are you going through a dark season? Trust God, have faith, and keep going forward. God has got your life all sorted out, and sooner than you think it will be revealed.

Like Tamar, retain your faith. Choose not to let your spirit be crushed. She knew what she wanted, whether Er sustained her or not, whether Onan supported her or not, whether her father-in-law approved of her or not. Her heart was fixed on what she wanted which she had been chosen for and had been planted by God in her – Her seed.

No situation has the capacity to bring you to a reversal.

I don't know what your dreams are. It may look like all of Earth is conspiring to kill that dream. God is looking to you to birth the seed that will bruise the head of the serpent in your community, country, and world. There is a service to humanity within you that must find expression. There are businesses in you that must be birthed.

If Tamar was able to birth what was in her against all odds, my prayer for you is that you will birth that business, that ministry, will bring forth that child, and you will celebrate the birth of your vision. Like Tamar who became a great-great-grandmother of David, you are a queen mother and no one will take your place.

Chapter 2

ISOLATION

Then said Judah to Tamar his daughter in law, Remain a widow at thy father's house...
Gen. 38:11

The instruction from Judah had been simple. Tamar was to return to her father's home and remain there as a widow. She wasn't being released from his family or given room to probably go in a different direction and start life afresh, instead she was to remain a widow and stay mourning in her father's house. This was to be her identity and she was to maintain it.

Is this familiar? Are there negative circumstances which have occurred in our lives that have become our label or the titles by which we are identified? *She's a barren woman. He's a divorcee. She's the one who has lost one job after the other. He's the one with a prison record. She was a former drug addict. He is an over-mature single.* Irrespective of labels the world seeks to define you by, you alone have the power to determine what name you should be called and the power to define your circumstances. While the world may have a name for you, God also has a name for you. That should be your constant refrain and your personal identity. Speak it to yourself and speak it to the world. "I am who God says I am."

Judah labelled Tamar with something negative. As far as he was concerned, there was something in her responsible for the deaths of his sons.

> *Then said Judah to Tamar his daughter in law, Remain a widow at thy father's house, till Shelah my son be grown: for he said, Lest peradventure he die also, as his brethren did. And Tamar went and dwelt in her father's house.*
> **Gen. 38:11**

While the world may have a name for you, God also has a name for you.

His negative perception of her caused him to do what many would do usually: put her far. Her 'ill luck' needed to be kept away from him and his family so she wouldn't bring in more evil. The place chosen by Judah for her, therefore, was widowhood.

This was where she was sent into.

I imagine the plan may have been that in putting her away she would disappear, become nothing, be extinct, fade away. She would be buried by her sorrows, become an old maid, or maybe eventually die suddenly. Judah felt sending her away had taken care of her. He may have hoped he wouldn't have to see her anymore.

Tamar went into widowhood and into isolation. What she didn't know was that she needed that time away to be prepared for the place God had created for her. Those who mocked didn't know there was a vision God had of her long before time began, and now the word was about to be activated.

Isolation comes before a blessing. You can't be blessed in the crowd. It usually doesn't happen that way. It is in the innermost chamber that God anoints. Far away from the crowd.

The blessings of thy father have prevailed above the blessings of my progenitors unto the utmost bound of the everlasting hills: they shall be on the head of Joseph, and on the crown of the head of him ***that was separate*** *from his brethren.*
Gen. 49:26

And when thou comest thither, look out there Jehu the

son of Jehoshaphat the son of Nimshi, and go in, and ***make him arise up from among his brethren, and carry him to an inner chamber****; Then take the box of oil, and pour it on his head, and say, Thus saith the LORD, I have anointed thee king over Israel. Then open the door, and flee, and tarry not.*

2 Kin. 9:2-3

Can you imagine the look on the faces of Joseph's brothers as they looked at, interacted and talked with him while he was prime minister of Egypt? He was not the same person they knew. His forging took place away from his brethren. Jehu was called out from his associates, taken into an innermost chamber, anointed, and the purpose of God revealed to him. David spent time in the wilderness before being called out and anointed. After the ceremony, he was sent back again into the wilderness before his time came to be anointed king.

Before God will anoint you, he will first separate you. This isn't peculiar to you and your circumstances alone but is the trademark for everyone to whom Heaven's assignment is attached. Do not fear isolation. It is the time needed to learn the patterns of Heaven, recognize God in the stillness, and have Him download His nature and His purpose into your being. When you finally 'show up', you are not the same person the world knew.

It is in the innermost chamber that God anoints. Far away from the crowd.

You cannot develop your voice in the midst of a crowd. This happens in the Secret Place. Before the fullness of the blessing tied to your destiny can come upon you, you must first be separated to Him.

Verily, verily, I say unto you, Except a corn of wheat fall into the ground and die, it abideth alone: but if it die, it bringeth forth much fruit.
Joh. 12:24

When you are in isolation you feel like you are in darkness, and no one is with you. This is the same feeling that comes with the buried and hidden seed. Like Tamar you wonder, *Have I been buried alive by circumstances? What sort of season is this?* Don't fret. The season of isolation is for your glorification and for your promotion. Not for your disgrace.

It is not possible for a child of God to be sabotaged by the enemy. When the enemy attempts to sabotage a child of God, one sold out completely to God, he ends up sabotaging himself. If the enemy had known what would have happened while trying to destroy Jesus, he would have left Him alone.

Which none of the princes of this world knew: for had they known it, they would not have crucified the Lord of glory.
1 Cor. 2:8

When we are isolated and we feel time is being wasted, the world is passing us by, or we are losing ground, what we do in those times determines what happens after the isolation. What we engage in during times we are thrust into isolation is what determines our acceleration when it is over.

Communion with the Holy Spirit is the key.

When Jesus caused his disciples to depart from him, they left him behind on the mountain.

And straightway Jesus constrained his disciples to get into a ship, and to go before him unto the other side, while he sent the multitudes away. And when he had sent the multitudes away, he went up into a mountain apart to pray: and when the evening was come, he was there alone. But the ship was now in the midst of the sea, tossed with waves: for the wind was contrary. And in the fourth watch of the night Jesus went unto them, walking on the sea.
Mat. 14:22-25

In that time Jesus was alone, things happened which made

all the difference in Him and to His world. The others who had gone far and were in a boat on the sea saw him walking towards them on the water! He had caught up with them though they had started way ahead of him - six whole hours ahead and in a vessel which many rowed! He was alone and had no vessel. In his time of isolation, he had made God His vehicle and was carried by the Spirit on superior technology which had collapsed time and processes for him!

Communion with the Holy Spirit is the key. It doesn't matter how far you think the competition has left you. It may be time to retreat into isolation to commune with the Holy Ghost for strategies that will accelerate you until you overtake.

Chapter 3

SEASONS

And in process of time the daughter of Shuah Judah's wife died; and Judah was comforted, and went up unto his sheepshearers to Timnath, he and his friend Hirah the Adullamite. And it was told Tamar, saying, Behold thy father in law goeth up to Timnath to shear his sheep.
Gen. 38:12-13

Tamar had settled in and adjusted to life in her father's house. I imagine when all the questions had been asked, tears had been shed, and pity-parties held, she still had routines she had to follow like every other woman. She awoke when they awoke, worked as they worked, shared meals with her family, and went to bed as they did. It was the same process day in day out.

This was a very difficult period. I imagine many questions

being asked of her and present within her heart.

What is the plan? She had no answer.

How long will this period last? She had no answer.

What can you do to change things? She had no answer.

Is there a way to hasten the process, or do you know someone who can do something about this? She had no answer.

Isn't this how our wilderness experiences feel? We cannot clearly define or understand what season we are in. But God can. When you come to the end of yourself and have no help, no hope, no wisdom, no one, this is God wanting you to recognize Him and give Him room to do what only He can, so that at the end no one - not even you - can take the glory.

We cannot clearly define or understand what season we are in. But God can.

The purpose of the wilderness is to refine you and produce from you the person God intends for the throne. But this refinement can only take place when you have the right attitude. In the famous words of a minister, "Your attitude determines your altitude." What are you involved in during your dark seasons? Are you trusting God and maintaining your praise like David did in the wilderness, or are you complaining, mourning, playing the victim? The right attitude is needed to bring you through. This is key. A positive attitude is important.

Though Tamar might have been in a pitiable situation and instructed to remain a widow, yet she didn't despair, feel sorry for herself, or put on an aura of mourning. She must have stayed so positive that someone felt comfortable enough to say to her, "Hey Tamar, your father-in-law is going up to Timnath to shear his sheep." If she was depressed I am sure she would have been left to abide alone and the information may have been withheld from her. No one engages a depressed person if they can avoid doing so.

Usually, especially when you have walked faithfully with God through the years, the enemy would not come with obvious attacks. His quintessential stock-in-trade for believers who genuinely love the Lord is depression because he knows if he can take away your will to fight he can hold you down. We are to be on our guard against depression.

One key way to fight depression is to praise. Here is what the Bible says:

> *Ye shall have a song, as in the night when a holy solemnity is kept; and gladness of heart, as when one goeth with a pipe to come into the mountain of the LORD, to the mighty One of Israel. And the LORD shall cause his glorious voice to be heard, and shall shew the lighting down of his arm, with the indignation of his*

anger, and with the flame of a devouring fire, with scattering, and tempest, and hailstones.
Isa. 30:29-30

You desire for God to speak, step in, and show Himself strong in your life. But He says first you shall have a song. You shall have gladness of heart. It is then that God's voice can be heard. Praise should always be your heart's response in whatever situation you find yourself. I am not saying it is *easy* or you will *feel* like praising. It can be a huge battle, but Your heart must have a song.

The purpose of the wilderness is to refine you and produce from you the person God intends for the throne.

Please be encouraged. Come to the throne one more time with a song, and soon His voice will be heard. If Joseph had been miserable and full of lamentations in prison, if his constant refrain had been, "This is such a bad country. Everyone is suffering as I am. What a bad world", would he have noticed what was happening with the butler and the baker? If he had been wallowing in self-pity he would not have cared what happened to others.

And Joseph came in unto them in the morning, and looked upon them, and, behold, they were sad. And he asked Pharaoh's officers that were with him in the ward of his lord's house, saying, Wherefore look ye so sadly to day? And they said unto him, We have dreamed a dream, and there is no interpreter of it. And Joseph said unto them, Do not interpretations belong to God? tell me them, I pray you.

Gen. 40:6-8

Are these words not amazing? His body was imprisoned but the real man - his spirit and soul (mind, will, emotions) - was free. He was expected to walk in despair, but he acted like the story was not yet over. He was called a slave, but he acted like a leader and ignored his prevailing circumstance to care for another. He was all alone in a foreign land, but he embraced others. Because of his attitude, I believe, God stepped in, brought him up, and placed him on a throne prepared for him.

The right attitude is needed to bring you through.

Returning our attention to our protagonist Tamar. Judith Hauptman, a Talmudic and Rabbinical expert says,

"At this point, the text reverts to Tamar, who had returned to her father's home. Verse 13 says that 'it

> *was reported to her that her father-in-law had gone up to Timnah for a sheep-shearing.' Both traditional and modern commentators skip over this seemingly simple verse. I find that it calls out for interpretation.*
>
> *My question is not who told Tamar that her father-in-law had gone to a sheep-shearing, but rather why people provided her with this information. The verse seems to suggest that there was general sympathy on the part of the local community for her plight. There she was, twice widowed, promised to the third son, but not permitted to perform levirate marriage with him even though he was now an adult. The townspeople, therefore, are likely to be suggesting to her that she take her fate into her own hands, that she clarify her ambiguous marital status.*
>
> *Note that they refer to Judah not by name but as her father-in-law, an ironic appellation since he clearly was not fulfilling his role of father-in-law for her." (www.jtsa.edu/judah-and-tamar-writing-the-story)*

Tamar may have had the empathy or at least sympathy of the townsfolk, was obviously well-liked enough to access this key piece of information and, as this professor speculates, popular opinion in the town may have been on her side. Her past husbands were wicked men and it seemed only Judah, their father, was oblivious to this fact. Others may have suspected their judgement had God's hand in it, and if this was not bad enough, her father-in-law had further gravely wronged her by refusing to solve the problem and thrown her into limbo. Yet she had stayed chaste.

Like Tamar, you may be experiencing hard or unexpected times. Remember you are just *passing through.* Watch your words and attitude in tough situations. This will determine the tenure of your wilderness sojourn.

Tamar heard Judah was coming to shear sheep. We will never know why this information was passed on to her. Was it meant to stir up a conversation, a pity-party, or remind her of her situation? Rub it in her face?

I imagine someone else receiving this same information. "Have you heard? The Judah who disgraced you, didn't give you his grown son Shelah and sent you back home is coming around. What are you going to do about it?" Isn't that how fights are stirred up and rash decisions taken? Naturally, they would want you to either insult Judah, sit in a pity-party

Watch your words and attitude in tough situations.

analysing all he did, or sink deeper in pain and isolation remembering all you went through.

But people of destiny use information differently. They hear what others hear but extract different value from the information. They know what to do with information received. Tamar was different. The words meant something different to her. What she learnt was not just for frivolous consumption. It was vital information.

Her unusual response was a reflection of her heart. She sat with others and walked as they did, but her heart was set on a different destination. As a result, when the information came, all she thought of was the longing within her that never left - bearing *her* seed.

In one of the books in this series, we discuss how Naomi was privy to general information.

And now is not Boaz of our kindred, with whose maidens thou wast? Behold, he winnoweth barley to night in the threshingfloor.

Rut. 3:2

This information which everyone knew became the perfect catalyst to move Ruth, one of the women listed in the genealogy of Christ, to the place designed for her. This also was experienced by Rahab.

And Joshua the son of Nun sent out of Shittim two men to spy secretly, saying, Go view the land, even Jericho. And they went, and came into an harlot's house, named Rahab, and lodged there. And it was told the king of Jericho, saying, Behold, there came men in hither to night of the children of Israel to search out the country.
Josh. 2:1-2

News of the spies' arrival was received by everyone in the city. Everyone, including the king. Yet, only Rahab and her family were spared because she knew how to utilize the news she had received. She was also grafted into the lineage of Christ.

Are we given to listening, not just to what is being said but to what isn't being said? Or are we given to flippancy? How do we handle information received? Finally, when we choose to respond, are our responses determined by general opinion?

When people of destiny get information, it becomes a revelation.

When people of destiny get information, it becomes a revelation. They ask, *What do I do with what I have heard?* Each day we would be privy to information that may have the potential to move us up to the next level. Do not get lost or carried away by the things around you. It would be disastrous and great folly to miss out on where you should be headed because you are flippant or want to please or appease men. We each have our individual race to run. Let God guide you daily.

Chapter 4

THE GARMENTS OF YOUR FUTURE

And she put her widow's garments off from her, and covered her with a vail, and wrapped herself...
Gen. 38:14

Tamar received news that Judah was going up to Timnath with a friend to shear sheep. She acknowledged the information and did two things. First, she unveiled herself, removing her old covering. Secondly, she re-veiled herself, putting on a different covering. These two points are very powerful and I will like us to explore each in great detail.

UNVEILING

And she put her widow's garments off from her...
Gen. 38:14

In ancient Israel, your garments clearly stated who you were. Lepers had their ‘uniforms’, same as priests. The rich were clearly seen to be rich, while the poor had fabrics they had access to within their income bracket. A veil was not just a covering for the head but represented an identity. You were what your clothes said you were.

Tamar’s veil represented her identity. It was a covering representing her mental patterns, standards, paradigms, and strongholds. Like her, we all wear a form of veil. These are the lenses through which we view and construct our models of engagement with life. These lenses determine our belief systems. If we wear rose-tinted lenses, everything we see is covered with a hint of red. If we wear dark lenses, no matter how bright it is in a room, our sight becomes dimmer.

Our lenses cause us not to see accurately. While the reality remains unchanged and untainted, our perceptions are. As a result, our perceptions become reality, govern our lives, constrain us, and determine our choices and lifestyle. We hold on to these perceptions tenaciously for different reasons:

perhaps they profit us, we truly believe in them, perhaps they are ingrained by force of habit, or they have been passed on to us by others, parents or other authority figures, and we have chosen to accept them.

Tamar was attired with the garment of widowhood. It was her covering, her identity, the way she was seen by others. It had been foisted on her through circumstances and by the people in her world. It was not something she ever took off. Even if she went to a new terrain and no one knew her, the identity of widowhood would speak for her, either through her attire or someone who may have been privy to her history. It was her burden, it was her cross. She was not allowed by society to put it down.

There are garments placed on us by our circumstances or by others which we carry around consciously or unconsciously. We have become so accustomed to them or are too tired to argue with those who label us that we may not know when to put them off. No one or circumstance has the right to give you a name which you do not want to be called. You have the power to choose who you would be and what you would be called, irrespective of external

… our perceptions become reality, govern our lives, constrain us, and determine our choices and lifestyle.

circumstances.

Tamar refused to see herself through the lenses foisted on her. Through what lens do you see yourself? Through what lens do you see your business? Praying and asking are one thing. Most of us do a lot of these. But are we thinking? Seeing possibilities as God sees them? Seeing ourselves as God has spoken? That desire or dream should never be an image you can't conceive. Your mind must grasp it before you can evolve into it.

> *Now unto him that is able to do exceeding abundantly above all that we* ***ask or think,*** *according to the power that worketh in us, Unto him be glory in the church by Christ Jesus throughout all ages, world without end. Amen.*
> **Eph. 3:20**

Tamar recognized something was about to happen in this season she was in. And this would not occur if she still carried the veil of widowhood around with her. She had to put it off. This was venturing beyond her comfort zone. But if she was ever going to be known as anything but 'Tamar the widow', then the widow's veil had to go. Are there ideals or opinions we hold on to which may have become obsolete in a new season?

Naomi told Ruth to go meet with Boaz. First, she had to wash, perfume herself, look different. Joseph was comfortable with his beard in prison, this was his identity and pride as a Hebrew. But when he was to be brought before the king, he shaved his beard and changed his clothes before heeding the call. Let's understand this.

The beard to the Hebrew man was symbolic of his identity and later instituted into law by God. It wasn't a symbol of fashion or an optional choice. When David's messengers had one-half of their beards shaved in 2 Samuel 10:4-5, he asked his ambassadors to wait in Jericho and not come back to the capital till their beards (and by extension their pride) grew back.

> *Wherefore Hanun took David's servants, and shaved off the one half of their beards, and cut off their garments in the middle, even to their buttocks, and sent them away. When they told it unto David, he sent to meet them, because the men were greatly ashamed: and the king said, Tarry at Jericho* ***until your beards be grown****, and then return.*

The Egyptians, on the other hand, abhorred facial hair and were always clean-shaven. Joseph chose to put off his pride by letting go of the beard when he was to come before an Egyptian king. Why? He realised that regardless of what his beard meant to him, it had no value to the one who summoned him. The old paradigm would serve no purpose and would be of no profit to him.

What if he had come before Pharaoh unchanged because he believed, like many, he should be accepted as he was? Or that he had a right to his fundamental human right of self-expression? I believe his idea would have been approved of, taken, and given to another who would execute it. Simply because he wasn't culture fit.

Isn't that what happens to many with their ideas? You come before an authority figure capable of promoting you and your proposal. He knows your idea is good, but he takes a look at you and you just don't look like someone who has the capacity to execute such ideas. Perhaps it is even obvious from your body language that you are not willing to make adjustments, after all, "This is who I am. This is my culture. They need to respect my traditions. I follow the money. Who cares about their patronage? The adjustment needs to come from the one needing my services." Isn't that what some of us say?

What are you holding on to that is impeding your moving forward? It is time to throw off that which is unprofitable to you in this season. Do not let your circumstances define you or be the narrative you carry around. Discard what you are holding on to which is irrelevant, ill-fitting, or even abhorrent in that place the Lord is taking you to.

Throw off unprofitable paradigms. Prepare yourself for

where you are going and not where you are coming from. If need be, you may need to repackage some parts of your identity where necessary. You must smell like it. You must sound like it. You must look like it. You must prepare yourself for your future, and not your past.

The only thing that should not be put away is the word and will of God. But if it emanates from man, it's a tradition, custom, or norm of man, it is not sacrosanct and can be subject to change. Your choices should not be built on cultural ideologies or popular belief. You should constantly realign yourself with God's purpose for your life by asking, *What does the Word say? What is God's word to me right now?*

RE-VEILING

...and covered her with a vail, and wrapped herself...
Gen. 38:14

A new season had come. Tamar recognised it was possible something was about to happen. What was her response? She put off her old veil and put on another, one she had never worn before. It was a new persona but was fitting for the terrain she needed to walk in. The purpose of her new veil? To meet Judah.

There is a veil for every new season. As the Bible says,

> *The wind bloweth where it listeth, and thou hearest the sound thereof, but canst not tell whence it cometh, and whither it goeth: so is every one that is born of the Spirit.*
> **Joh. 3:8**

There is a veil for every new season.

The man or woman led by God is an enigma. You cannot tell what he or she is able to do. In business, you should constantly be open to change. At your job, you should deliver surprising results, and go beyond the norm. You should be one led by the Spirit and non-predictable.

Tamar didn't just throw off her garments of widowhood and say, "What do I wear now? What are other people putting on? What else is appealing to me?" No. There was a covering strategically designed for the specific individual she was going to meet. She received it within her spirit and put it on. Her 'veil' was tailored to meet the need in the one she was to encounter.

A tiny note here. Dressing is really about what is appropriate to the occasion. Swimming trunks are appropriate at the pool but not the board room. Every garment has its time, place, and occasion.

Isn't it interesting that she veiled herself like a harlot? While she wasn't dressed to expose her body, her veil and clothing marked her out as someone in that trade. This is food for thought. There is more to decent dressing than being covered. Like Tamar, even when we are covered, who are we channelling? She was covered from her head to her toe such that Judah didn't even see her face, but Tamar was channelling a harlot. There's clearly more to an individual's persona than the attires or garments displayed.

There is a key, relevant information, and strategy meant to move you to the next level and for your promotion in every season - whether it is to grow a career or business. You cannot depend on speculations, mental calculations, or market surveys. It takes only the wisdom received from God to know what strategy you need as you venture into every circumstance and every situation the Lord will bring you to.

Joseph prepared specifically when leaving prison to get Pharaoh's attention. Esther prepared specifically to get the king's approval when preparing to meet him. She couldn't have entered in through her wisdom irrespective of how beautiful she was. She was guided into it by Hegai, the one with experience about the king, the keeper of the king's women.

Until we are willing to put on lenses that allow us to see all the new level demands, our minds cannot grasp possibilities, see them as real and tangible, and cause them to manifest into reality.

Chapter 5

THE PURSUIT OF DESTINY

...and sat in an open place, which is by the way to Timnath; for she saw that Shelah was grown, and she was not given unto him to wife.

Gen. 38:14

Have you ever known intensely within your spirit you are carrying a vision that it causes you to become restless? Have you ever been so conscious of the reality of the intangible that you behave as if what is not seen is already in your possession? Has your attitude ever been quite incongruous with your reality? I understand what this feels like.

While I respect and honour all men and women, and that is regardless of how old they may be, not ever am I intimidated by any, even from when I was as little as three. This was how I was raised. I am steeped in this belief - to respect all men but fear none. The same way I comported myself with audacious faith in God when I was 22 is the way I was in my forties.

In retrospect, I imagine now how difficult I must have been to stomach for those who preferred to intimidate young people on sheer account of how old they were. I was just so sure that God was in me and with me that it was impossible to be intimidated. While I may not have been confident in myself, my confidence in God was sure. I remain sure of His lovingkindness, sure mercies, and unfailing goodness. I know *Whom* I have believed. Tough times may come but He always comes through.

Tamar had abided in her father's house all these years, a poster girl for the season of contradiction. Her years in isolation had not dulled her dream. Instead, the retreat had sharpened her vision. All through the years, she observed Judah and his family from afar, watching and waiting for Shelah to be grown.

When he was man enough, she didn't return and remind them that she was to be married to him. Perhaps the patriarchal culture did not allow her to speak up. It is safe to say that her reputation and the events of the past were enough to disqualify her. Instead, she waited and waited to be summoned. But it never happened. She realized it probably never would. She had respected and trusted Judah but he had not kept his word. In fact, Hebrew scriptures allude to the fact that Judah may have 'regretted' promising Shelah to Tamar.

Tamar had to be free of Judah's family by bearing a child for her late husband. In contemporary times we can't relate to this, but apparently it was the levirate law of marriage. Her cohabiting with Judah would only be for this purpose - raising seed to Er's name, thus causing her to discharge her duty to the household of Judah. Judith Hauptman explains:

> *"She also knew that once she bore a child with Judah as the father, her ties to his family would dissolve and she could then marry whomever she pleased (or perhaps remain with Judah)."*
> *(www.jtsa.edu/judah-and-tamar-writing-the-story)*

What kept Tamar determined that this lineage was where she was going to fulfil her vision and birth her seed? I wonder if, beyond fulfilling the law, she sensed in her spirit a blessing was coming over this family? We see many years later Israel speaking over Judah and promising him that the Messiah would come through his lineage.

> *Judah, thou art he whom thy brethren shall praise: thy hand shall be in the neck of thine enemies; thy father's*

children shall bow down before thee. Judah is a lion's whelp: from the prey, my son, thou art gone up: he stooped down, he couched as a lion, and as an old lion; who shall rouse him up?

Kingdom people do not take on jobs, they accept assignments.

The sceptre shall not depart from Judah, nor a lawgiver from between his feet, until Shiloh come; and unto him shall the gathering of the people be. Binding his foal unto the vine, and his ass's colt unto the choice vine; he washed his garments in wine, and his clothes in the blood of grapes: His eyes shall be red with wine, and his teeth white with milk.

Gen. 49:8-12

No this was not about having babies. This was way beyond that. This was about destiny. For you too, you should not just see as the carnal man: *A business or job is just for making money and keeping body and soul together. Marriage is occurring because one is at a certain age.* No. Everything we do must be about destiny. Kingdom people do not take on jobs, they accept assignments. We seek first the kingdom of God and His righteousness in all these legitimate pursuits.

Greater risks mean potentially greater rewards.

But seek ye first the kingdom of God, and his righteousness; and all these things shall be added unto you.
Matthew 6:33

When we take on the Kingdom agenda and our businesses become a vehicle for Kingdom finance, when the marriage becomes a force for the Kingdom, we will be sure to see fresh dimensions open up to birth the extraordinary from the ordinary.

RISK AND REWARD

Now Tamar had on a new veil and a new paradigm, she was not waiting for change to happen to her. She needed to move from her present location and rise to the path of purpose. She was going to make change happen.

It is time to move forward. You cannot remain in the same position when your paradigm has shifted. Inner transformation would force a relocation in your life. A new mindset, new decisions which would dictate new habits, and new actions will literally reconstruct your circumstances to align with what your mind conceives.

For as he thinketh in his heart, so is he.
Pro. 23:7

Some individuals may need to return to formal education to take some courses. It may be a long or short one. You may need to repackage your business or your physical appearance. You cannot remain where you have been once you receive illumination. Tamar's transformation was not for where she was. Her transformation propelled her to a new location. She arose in her new veil and moved towards purpose.

Leaving your comfort zone can be risky. If it will not require divine intervention then I can safely say God is not involved. In Tamar's case this was true. It would have had her killed if she was discovered. She would have been stoned to death for playing the harlot. How could she prove that she intended to simply meet with her father-in-law? If she was caught it would have seemed like a tall tale. Fortunately, her risk paid off.

Great risks mean potentially great rewards. The greater the risk of any venture, however, the fewer people dare it and the fewer the competition. The fewer the competition, the greater your reward. A warning though. While we take strategic risks in business, there should be a mitigant in place. As in Ponzi schemes, if it's too good to be true, it probably is.

Chapter 6

LOCATION AND CONTRACTUAL OBLIGATIONS

And he turned unto her by the way, and said, Go to, I pray thee, let me come in unto thee; (for he knew not that she was his daughter in law.) And she said, What wilt thou give me, that thou mayest come in unto me? And he said, I will send thee a kid from the flock. And she said, Wilt thou give me a pledge, till thou send it? And he said, What pledge shall I give thee? And she said, Thy signet, and thy bracelets, and thy staff that is in thine hand. And he gave it her...

Gen. 38:16-18

Tamar had arrived at the place where she was sure Judah would pass through, a place on the road to Timnath. Though covered with a veil, she chose an open place where he could see her easily. She had to be strategic about being seen, and ensure Judah saw her. I imagine she might have tried to find the exact time he would pass by.

In business, location is extremely important. You need to be located where you can be easily accessed by your target market. This is beyond a physical location. Virtual and digital access is also key these days. In fact, many businesses are closing their physical locations and moving to purely digital businesses.

I know a few women who never ever seem to answer their phones. This is such a problem. How do clients reach you? Do you expect them to all show up physically at your outlet or office? Your phones must always be manned. Some women toss their business phones around so carelessly their toddlers answer incoming calls. "Heyyo? U ah u (Hello, who are you?) My mummy is in the bathroom!" If the corporate client is a man that may be the last time he calls. Another may think, *If her toddler answers her phones maybe she would conduct my own contract with the same lack of diligence.* We are evaluated on seemingly little details.

Tamar was now in the researched location. She was in position and everything was set. This was dangerous. While she knew she had done all she could, as with all ventures that lead to destiny, this would need God's help. If he didn't help her she would be dead.

Finally, Judah shows up. It is too late to change her plan. She is in a prostitute's garb in public. She sees him through the veil and waits with bated breath, many thoughts going through her mind, especially understanding she was actually looking at her father-in-law coming down the road. As she stands still, watching, heart beating, a part of her wonders what she is really doing here, suddenly wishing she could return home. She has no idea how things would play out.

While all these thoughts are rushing through her mind, God intervenes: Judah stops, turns aside from his path, and meets with her.

"WHAT WILL YOU GIVE ME…?"

When Judah saw her, he thought her to be an harlot; because she had covered her face. And he turned unto her by the way, and said, Go to, I pray thee, let me come in unto thee; (for he knew not that she was his daughter in law.)

Gen. 38:15-16

Judah didn't realize the woman before him was his daughter-in-law. He negotiated with her even though he had no form of payment on him. When he made a promise to pay afterwards, she asked him "What will you give me?" She wanted a token which would serve as a guarantee of payment.

A lot of the time indiscretion truncates destiny.

And he turned unto her by the way, and said, Go to, I pray thee, let me come in unto thee; (for he knew not that she was his daughter in law.) And she said, What wilt thou give me, that thou mayest come in unto me? And he said, I will send thee a kid from the flock. And she said, Wilt thou give me a pledge, till thou send it? And he said, What pledge shall I give thee? And she said, Thy signet, and thy bracelets, and thy staff that is in thine hand. And he gave it her, and came in unto her, and she conceived by him.

Gen. 38:16-18

Insisting on a token, she asked for his signet (his identity and his seal), his bracelets (his display of wealth), and his staff (his support and strength). These are modern-day equivalents of a passport, driver's license, social security number, credit cards, fingerprints, and birth certificate. Yet, Judah was so consumed with his desire that he gave this strange woman *everything* she asked for.

Let's examine each symbol closely.

His Signet

In ancient times, every man's signet or ring was unique to him. It was his signature before writing became widespread. Even after writing became commonplace, scribes would draft documents for most business transactions and a signet would then be pressed into a piece of wax on the document. This was the seal of authenticity unique to the owner of the ring (signet) which could not be faked.

Judah's signet was his identity, and if that signet was not in his possession he couldn't transact any business or buy land. This was a grave decision. In Mesopotamia, the loss of one's seal resulted in the annulment of ALL legal agreements tied to that seal, thus resulting in the invalidation of forged documents on which that seal appeared.

Judah's signet was his endorsement. An endorsement is not just for documents. People, products, and services are endorsed. Zagat ratings are assigned to restaurants, Michelin stars to chefs. In most industries endorsers rule the roost, especially in industries where value delivered is subjective, e.g.

acting, music, architecture, the culinary arts, literature, and writing, art. Gatekeepers decide who is who.

The ability to receive a seal of approval or endorsement in our fields after we have done our best is usually determined by the favour of the Lord and of endorsers. When we have the opportunity to access endorsers, this favour becomes directly linked to our ability to recognise, honour, and be receptive to these endorsers. It doesn't matter how amazing everyone else thinks the painting is. Until the endorsers say You Are, you can't say I Am. There's no point in trying to pray them away.

What is your relationship with your endorsers? Daniel had favour in the eyes of Ashpenaz, the prince of the eunuchs in Babylon.

Now God had brought Daniel into favour and tender love with the prince of the eunuchs.
Daniel 1:9

Hegai, also, who was a 'gatekeeper' in the king's palace was also the one who gave Esther the key to the king's heart.

So it came to pass, when the king's commandment and his decree was heard, and when many maidens were gathered together unto Shushan the palace, to the custody of Hegai, that Esther was brought also unto the king's house, to the custody of Hegai, keeper of the women. And the maiden pleased him, and she obtained kindness of him; and he speedily gave her her things for purification, with such things as belonged to her, and seven maidens, which were meet to be given her, out of the king's house: and he preferred her and her maids unto the best place of the house of the women.

Esther 2:8-9

Tamar received Judah's endorsement and seal which she couldn't have accessed through normal means. This could only have occurred through the help of the Lord.

His Bracelets

Judah's jewellery were a sign of how wealthy he was and his status in society. They were of immense value and had monetary value. It was also a means by which he could be recognised and identified.

His Staff

A man's staff signifies

- His identity: Most staffs were carved uniquely for the

owner.

- His authority: Many rulers had staffs which symbolised their leadership, power, and rulership.
- His status: Men of high status carried staffs even if they weren't a functional requirement.
- His physical support system: It aided his mobility.
- His defence: It was used when offended and in defence of oneself.

Doesn't Tamar's demands strike you as odd? She was asking for items that struck at the core of his identity. I wonder what she was thinking.

Immorality will collect from you what is valuable.

Was it not even more odd that Judah acceded to her requests? Was he under a spell? Or … was this who he was? Were there things about him that she knew that made her so sure that if she veiled herself and sat where a harlot would normally sit, Judah was sure to come to her?

Immorality will collect from you what is valuable. It robs you of your God-given identity, robs you of wealth, and reduces you to a piece of bread.

For by means of a whorish woman a man is brought to a

piece of bread: and the adulteress will hunt for the precious life.
Pro. 6:26

Perhaps she was sending a subtle message to her father-in-law. Everything she was doing was so he could perform the rites of the nearest kinsman in the stead of her late husband, thus honouring the law. But his desire was just to spend some time with a harlot. In this instance, she was more righteous than he was.

THE IMPORTANCE OF LEVERAGE

If Tamar had not collected those items from Judah, but had tried to negotiate with him after he had his way, she would have had to make do with whatever he decided he would part with. In the first book in this series, we explored the power of leverage through the life of Rahab, a harlot who understood this principle.

Rahab had invited the spies up to her roof, showed them there was enough flax to protect them and make them comfortable for the night, and had then left them alone. Some hours later, after having proved her capacity to deliver the value they desired, she comes up to the roof before they can extract real value from the transaction and states exactly what her 'fees' would be. Everything she asked for she received.

Show interested parties what you have to offer. For goods that can be tested or tasted, like catering services, give a sample where necessary. Isn't it interesting how we end up buying the whole product after partaking of taste samples offered in places like Costco and Sam's Club? Offer samples. When they express their desire for the full package, ask for a token.

I believe Joseph possessed everything except this leverage. He provided answers to the butler and baker, and even made his plea, "Do not forget me." But the butler still did.

And he restored the chief butler unto his butlership again; and he gave the cup into Pharaoh's hand: But he hanged the chief baker: as Joseph had interpreted to them. Yet did not the chief butler remember Joseph, but forgat him.

Gen. 40:21-28

Besides his plea Joseph made no specific demands, so he could not be remembered. He was forgotten for two years. Despite his being highly anointed, he was forgotten because he couldn't leverage his gifts.

Thank God for sending a dream to Pharaoh. The butler then remembered Joseph's role in his life (I doubt it was the first time). He must have been insensitive, selfish, and an ingrate. He was probably one of those who always want to know, "What is in it for me?"

If the butler had the capacity to forget Joseph the first time, he may not have introduced Joseph at this time for Joseph's sake. He may have made the introductions for his own selfish gain. Perhaps he knew Pharaoh would be happy he brought in a solution provider on this relevant issue and he would then find himself in Pharaoh's good books. He had no way of knowing the introduction would have such far-reaching consequences.

You can only negotiate for what you want when you have the leverage. Check where the balance of power is in every transaction before you begin negotiations.

Chapter 7

THE POWER OF SILENCE

… And he gave it her, and came in unto her, and she conceived by him. And she arose, and went away, and laid by her vail from her, and put on the garments of her widowhood.

Gen. 38:18-19

This chapter leads me to the salient issue of discretion. I am certain Tamar could not have shared her plans with anyone. No one, not even those she was so close to, would have agreed with her as this was too risky. This would be certain death if she was discovered. Besides, if anyone else became privy to the information shared, she was in danger of exposure. Like I always say "Your best friend has a best friend who may not be *your* friend."

There are stages on our path to destiny when there is just no one we can or should confide in. This is a fact. We are certain in our spirit about what we have heard from God, but no other human can understand, irrespective of how close they may be to you. The ability to stay silent until the right time could be the determining factor for birthing or cutting off what has been promised.

Tamar dressed up and went to the place chosen to carry out her mission without sharing a word. She then returned to her home with the expensive items she had received from Judah and carefully hid them. She put on the attire by which she was identified and went about her duties while within her body conception occurred. Though she wore the garments of widowhood, the seed conceived within her was proof of her change of status in the spirit realm.

You may not look like your future right now; your garments may not match where you are headed yet. But within you is growing a seed that will change your story forever! It may be the seed of a solution mankind needs or of leadership. Whatever vision God had given you will defy every externally imposed garment and find expression.

Your best friend has a best friend who may not be your friend.

Tamar was definitely happy. Her quest was over and her prayers were now answered. Yet, despite her joy, she was silent. Joy is such a great temptation to discretion. Joy shared is joy doubled. It's really no fun rejoicing alone. Also, the symptoms of the first trimester of pregnancy can be arduous but she couldn't receive the help and kind attention she needed because she was silent. Some of us, in craving attention, sympathy, or out of excitement, spill the beans.

Loss of sympathy and attention are a small price to pay to birth destiny. The one on the way to fulfilling purpose is a person of discretion. Not everyone needs to know what God has revealed to you. Before the fall of Jericho, if Rahab had announced to her friends what she wanted to discuss with the spies, the opportunity to enter into a transaction with them may never have occurred. Also, after she had met with the spies, she was warned to be quiet.

And if thou utter this our business, then we will be quit of thine oath which thou hast made us to swear.

Jos. 2:20

This conversation was treason and could have been reported to the king who would have had all of them killed. Also, the opportunity to be free along with every member of her family would never have come to fruition.

A lot of the time indiscretion has the potential to truncate destiny. We can't talk about every idea before it is cooked or fully baked. For some of us, those close to us can't entrust us with important information. A person of destiny knows how to meditate over an issue for months and resist the temptation to share until the time has come to reveal it.

Most transactions are not completed until one critical principle is applied – silence as things work out. If you are uncomfortable with silence you may truncate transactions. If you can't wait patiently and let events unfold before you proactively intervene you may miss the best deal.

Not everyone needs to know what God has revealed to you.

Tamar had the ability to be still, brooding quietly for three months without saying a word. If she had spoken and revealed what she did, anything could have happened. But after a while her state could not be hidden, and the 'neighbourhood watch' reported to Judah.

And it came to pass about three months after, that it was told Judah, saying, Tamar thy daughter in law hath played the harlot; and also, behold, she is with child by whoredom. And Judah said, Bring her forth, and let her be burnt.

Gen. 38:24

Judah's hatred is revealed in his request immediately he heard the news. He doesn't interrogate her or care enough to treat her as a daughter but immediately asks that she be burnt. Wisdom had revealed who he could be to Tamar and this had taught her to be discrete. While being dragged to the stake, she revealed the identity of the father of her children.

> *When she was brought forth, she sent to her father in law, saying, By the man, whose these are, am I with child: and she said, Discern, I pray thee, whose are these, the signet, and bracelets, and staff. And Judah acknowledged them, and said, She hath been more righteous than I; because that I gave her not to Shelah my son. And he knew her again no more.*
>
> **Gen. 38:25-26**

Tamar didn't state Judah was the father of her children. She simply brought forth concrete proof of his identity - his signet, his staff, and his bracelets! What she did was a shadow of DNA tests in the future. This young lady brought out proof that no one but Judah could have given her.

Besides him, those close to him would also have recognised these items including his friend if he had been present, the Adullamite he had sent with a kid to give to 'the harlot'. Now the identity of this individual was finally revealed, Judah had to acknowledge that she had taken the right step since he didn't give her Shelah as he had promised.

Did the seed in Tamar finally speak? Yes, it did at the time ordained, when every contrary voice had been silenced.

And it came to pass in the time of her travail, that, behold, twins were in her womb. And it came to pass, when she travailed, that the one put out his hand: and the midwife took and bound upon his hand a scarlet thread, saying, This came out first. And it came to pass, as he drew back his hand, that, behold, his brother came out: and she said, How hast thou broken forth? this breach be upon thee: therefore his name was called Pharez. And afterward came out his brother, that had the scarlet thread upon his hand: and his name was called Zarah.

Gen. 38:27-30

Tamar didn't just become a mother to one child but to two sons, Zarah and Pharez.

Perhaps, like me, you have been wondering how Judah became the person we see afterwards in Genesis 44:18-34 interacting with Joseph in Egypt, ready to stake his life for his word and integrity.

Then Judah came near unto him, and said, Oh my lord, let thy servant, I pray thee, speak a word in my lord's ears, and let not thine anger burn against thy servant: for thou art even as Pharaoh. My lord asked his servants, saying, Have ye a father, or a brother? And we said unto my lord, We have a father, an old man, and a child of his old age, a little one; and his brother is dead, and he alone is left of his mother, and his father loveth him. And thou saidst unto thy servants, Bring him down unto me, that I may set mine eyes upon him.

And we said unto my lord, The lad cannot leave his father: for if he should leave his father, his father would die. And thou saidst unto thy servants, Except your youngest brother come down with you, ye shall see my face no more. And it came to pass when we came up unto thy servant my father, we told him the words of my lord. And our father said, Go again, and buy us a little food. And we said, We cannot go down: if our youngest brother be with us, then will we go down: for we may not see the man's face, except our youngest brother be with us. And thy servant my father said unto us, Ye know that my wife bare me two sons: And the one went out from me, and I said, Surely he is torn in pieces; and I saw him not since: And if ye take this also from me, and mischief befall him, ye shall bring down my gray hairs with sorrow to the grave.

Now therefore when I come to thy servant my father, and the lad be not with us; seeing that his life is bound up in the lad's life; It shall come to pass, when he seeth that the lad is not with us, that he will die: and thy servants shall bring down the gray hairs of thy servant our father with sorrow to the grave. For thy servant became surety for the lad unto my father, saying, If I bring him not unto thee, then I shall bear the blame to my father for ever.

Now therefore, I pray thee, let thy servant abide instead of the lad a bondman to my lord; and let the lad go up with his brethren. For how shall I go up to my father, and the lad be not with me? lest peradventure I see the evil that shall come on my father.

This was the same man who had been known to have no moral compass as was evidenced by his treatment of Joseph, his sons, and Tamar. He had sold his brother into slavery.

And Judah said unto his brethren, What profit is it if we slay our brother, and conceal his blood? Come, and let us sell him to the Ishmeelites, and let not our hand be upon him; for he is our brother and our flesh. And his brethren were content. Then there passed by Midianites merchantmen; and they drew and lifted up Joseph out of the pit, and sold Joseph to the Ishmeelites for twenty pieces of silver: and they brought Joseph into Egypt. And Reuben returned unto the pit; and, behold, Joseph was not in the pit; and he rent his clothes. And he returned unto his brethren, and said, The child is not; and I, whither shall I go?

Genesis 37:26–30

His word meant nothing when he promised Shelah to Tamar. He had raised two brute sons and still didn't know or acknowledge they were evil but blamed their innocent victim for their deaths. How are you unable to tell your sons have evil hearts, evil enough to be killed by God? How do you raise such sons?

Isn't it strange that just like has happened in time past, the children seemed to be replicating the sins of their father? Some mistakes Abraham made, Isaac his son also did. Same as Jacob. Also, Onan was selfish, greedy, envious of his brother, and coveted his inheritance. This was just like his father, Judah, who had hated his brother Joseph and conspired to kill him because he believed Joseph, based on his dreams, would receive an inheritance and legacy greater than his. This was a generational evil. Judah had then kept Tamar bound indefinitely to his family, neglecting to set her free or grant her freedom by letting her marry his last son.

This same man could also casually hand over very important tools of his identity to a veiled harlot he had just met for sensual pleasure. In a sense, Judah had lost his true identity completely. His having given his signet, staff, and bracelets to Tamar as collateral was only a physical acting-out of that reality. He was as cavalier as was Esau who traded his birthright for a bowl of food.

Yet, some years afterwards, we see Judah standing before Joseph in Egypt, eloquent, self-sacrificing, and compassionate, willing to stake his life on his word and integrity. A transformation had certainly occurred along the way. Tamar, though a victim and a woman in a patriarchal society, seemed to have played a critical role in his life. God makes her story an interruption in the Joseph narrative because it is critical that we understand what changed Judah's nature so radically.

God is at work in every pain, process, and path you have to go through.

This seemingly helpless but strategic and wise woman of vision caused Judah to acknowledge when she was to be burnt "She is more righteous than I." She forced him to confront his unrighteousness and repent, and her encounter with him prepared him to carry the weight of his destiny.

He is blessed that the one in whose hands he placed his fate was Tamar and not Jacob because she, who he had disqualified, was the one who caused him to be qualified. While Jacob took Esau's inheritance, Tamar unlocked his real identity and gave Judah his inheritance. Through Tamar and the seed she bore, Judah was grafted into the lineage of Jesus. One of her sons would become an ancestor of David and of the Christ!

Unknown to Tamar, this was what had been the purpose for all she went through all along. She would not just birth a child but would birth an ancestor of Christ. God is at work in every pain, process, and path you go through. Like Tamar, who made history and whose joy was complete, keep trusting Him and know without a shadow of doubt He will bring you through and cause your joy to be full.

CLOSING WORDS

Consider the size of a key relative to a door, how small it appears. Yet, it is superior to the door because no matter how solid, how heavy, or how great a door is, it turns on a key.

That problem may seem like a heavy door but all you need is the right key as not every key opens every door. You need the key for the door that stands between you and destiny. For us, irrespective of what we are faced with, wisdom or the relevant strategy is that key.

The Bible says about wisdom:

Wisdom is the principal thing; therefore get wisdom: and with all thy getting get understanding.

Pro. 4:7

The beautiful thing about wisdom is it not being gender-specific. Also, it can be utilized by everyone, irrespective of status or citizenship. While people of destiny know they have a past, they lay hold on wisdom and keep moving forward.

They choose not to be constrained or lose sight of the glorious future which they envision. They recognize that the past cannot be rewritten but do not make the future a victim or hostage of the past as it is a story waiting to be told. They choose to tell their stories and cause their past to become a platform of praise.

No matter how solid, how heavy, or how great a door is, it turns on a key.

Israel was a patriarchal, parochial, and strictly traditional society. When making a list of what you owned as a man at the time, it was usual to say, as an example, "I own four houses, two sheep, three camels, and two wives." Wives were deemed to be personal property and women valued less than men.

Yet these three women of destiny, Rahab, Ruth, and Tamar, who each applied and possessed distinct peculiar wisdom which was uncommon, refused to give up, broke the mould, and shattered the glass ceiling through their stories and the understandings they possessed. How much more possible is it today for us to blow up spiritual, physical, and societal boundaries imposed on us?

Today, our opportunities are limitless, and access to the new covenant provides us unrestrained, indefinable reach beyond what we ask, think, or imagine. That is God's promise.

Now unto him that is able to do exceeding
abundantly above all that we ask or think, according
to the power that worketh in us,
Eph. 3:20

I don't know your past, your struggles, what situation you are going through. But **choose** not to be held back. Go forward!

In the words of Martin Luther King,

If you can't fly run.
If you can't run walk.
If you can't walk crawl.
Whatever you do, keep moving.

Enough with the stories.

Leave the past and its failures behind.

Move on! Move on! Move on!

ABOUT THE AUTHOR

Olajumoke Adenowo (Arc) is a multiple award-winning architect with over three decades of industry experience. Described as Africa's 'Starchitect' and trailblazer when profiled by CNN and BBC, she is one of Africa's outstanding architects and the only female in this elite category. Christened the **Face of Architecture in Nigeria** by the Guardian, she has been featured in the world's foremost architectural journal Architectural Record and in Forbes Women and Fortune magazine.

In 2013, she was instituted into the Hall of Fame of **Personalities of Black Ancestry** by the University of West England, Bristol, among other global personalities of black heritage.

Olajumoke gained admission into Obafemi Awolowo University, Ile-Ife, at the age of fourteen, and she acquired the first distinction in Masters of Science in Architecture in the University's history. She is also an alumnus of a number of prestigious institutions including the Harvard Kennedy School of Government, the Yale School of Management, the IESE Business School amongst others. She is a member of the Institute of Chartered Arbitrators (UK) and a Fellow of the Nigerian Institute of Architects.

Olajumoke started her career at Femi Majekodunmi Associates, where she had the privilege of designing the Federal Ministry of Finance Headquarters in Abuja. In 1994, she founded her own multi-award-winning architecture firm, AD Consulting, which specialises also in the master planning of eco-sensitive developments. AD Consulting is Nigeria's most internationally awarded firm. She has been the principal partner from inception till date.

In 1999, Olajumoke's passion for raising transformational leaders led her to establish the faith-based philanthropy, Awesome Treasures Foundation. It is recognized by the United Nations and affiliated to the Edmond De Rothschild Foundation Family Philanthropy Platform. Awesome Treasures Foundation is established on three continents with initiatives impacting millions.

She is the pioneer recipient of the **New African Women in Business Award**, has been recognised as one of Africa's **'Top Ten Most Powerful Women in Business'**, one of **Nigeria's Most Inspiring Women**, one of Nigeria's **100 most Influential Nigerians**, the International Alliance for Women **World of Difference 100 Award**, as well as one of the **Most Inspiring Women in Nigeria** amongst other honours.

Olajumoke Adenowo was the recipient of the **2019 Leadership Award** by the Constituency For Africa

(Washington, DC). In 2019 she was appointed a visiting professor at Germany's Leading Architecture program, Technische Universitat Munchen (TUM) in Germany. She was honoured as a Laureate and Guest Scientist at the Chair of Theory, History of Architecture and Art & Design.

Adenowo is a speaker of note at summits and conferences, and has spoken at several global platforms, including the Global Women's Forum, Harvard Business School's Africa Business Club, Cambridge University's African Society, and SOLVE MIT's flagship conference for global thought leaders and innovators. She is also a minister of the gospel, and member of The International Coalition of Apostolic Leaders. She ministers to all genders and also young adults, raising transformational leaders, and has held over 120 Awesome Treasures Summits internationally, with attendees of up to 5000 at the youth summits.

Olajumoke has served on juries and panels of global initiatives such as The Cartier Initiative for Women Awards. She has authored several books, including *Life Spring, Mysterious Seed*, *Appointment With Destiny,* and *Beyond My Dreams*, and hosts her own syndicated radio program, Voice of Change on Leadership.

She is married to Olukorede and they are blessed with two men.

Printed in Great Britain
by Amazon

47299267R00061